YOU DIDN'T HEAR THIS FROM ME

A.L. Nielsen

YOU DIDN'T HEAR THIS FROM ME

A.L. Nielsen

ISBN-13: 978-0-9883891-7-5

Acknowledgments: Some of these poems first appeared in *Issue Number One*, *Nethula*, *Slave Speaks*, *Wooden Teeth*, *Gargoyle*, and *Yellow Field.*

Cover Design: Wendy Glaess
Typesetting: Steve Tills

theenk Books
107 Washington Street
Palmyra, New York 14522

Contact: theenkbooks@twc.com

To order: http://theenkBooks.com

Also distributed by Small Press Distribution
1341 Seventh StreetBerkeley, CA 94710
http://www.spdbooks.org

Also by A.L. Nielsen

Poetry

Heat Strings
Evacuation Routes
Stepping Razor
VEXT
Mixage
Mantic Semantic
A Brand New Beggar
Tray

Criticism

Reading Race
Writing between the Lines
C.L.R. James: A Critical Introduction
Black Chant
Integral Music

As Editor

Reading Race in American Poetry

Don't Deny My Name: Words and Music and the Black Intellectual Tradition, by Lorenzo Thomas

with Lauri Ramey

Every Goodbye Ain't Gone: An Anthology of Innovative Poetry by African Americans

What I Say: An Anthology of Innovative Poetry by Black Writers in America

CONTENTS

In Memoriam

David Bromige

"I can't read and here's a book."

Afar, our story chambered apartments
look like concrete harmonicas.
– Cathy Park Hong

I

from CHINA

Morning's moisture brings
Rabbit to my door

It's not his year

They asked me to tell them
All that I knew

It didn't take as long
As it took Lao Tzu

Carmen named herself
    For an opera

Wei Yan waits
    Listens
        For her name to sound

My name is no name
    In the street

Way a
Weigh on
Whey

Wu wei
I can not tell you

What was that I just heard

About the seven unmentionables

The dogs line up
To examine who
Would own them

Small
Fluffy

The dogs like that

Angry Birds

Have taken China by storm

Teaching Building #3

English
Through the leaves
Around the fish pond

In front the
Foreign Languages School
Where I am to speak

That same English
The fish attend

But the birds
Don’t translate

The morning after
Tasting his favorite dish
For the first time

I find the poet
Chairman Mao
At the tea stand

Busted

Carrying the Blues to Wuhan
We harped on it

Larry had said
My house would have
A round room

And in that room
Round Buddha
Laughing

But Buddha
Is tall and slender
Like Larry

Laughing still

Wake to the chirping of birds

Time to change their batteries

Mona Lisa
Mona Lisa

Sidewalked outside
Lucky Cakes

The artist bent
For benefice
At his work

Every blessed day another
Mona Lisa

White cat
Leashed
By parking
Lot attendant

No more to
Terrorize
The hotel
Greeters

Watching Mulan
In Wuhan

Subtitles
Subtending

Unending
Disney

Incessant rain
From the
Air

Conditioners
Far
Above

Signs taken for showers

The Tao
Runs
Hot and cold

American alfalfa
Has followed me here

Like chicken feet
To feed

Green jade
Dielectric
Crisp chicken
Abalone conquers

The World Cup
First day filled

Ceaseless rain

Wu Shang and Dixie
Good gawd

African China
In China

THE RULES

1)Be Respectful when rejecting. Many women will message you, but you'll only have time for a few.

2)Be Courteous. Our women are very aggressive to meet men like you. If it's too much, please say so kindly.

I dreamed I was awakened
By a Chinese silence

But it was just Wisconsin

So
It was
No
Dream

Row row row
Your boat
Gently

Streamed
From
The valley below

Down
In the valley
So low

Merrily Merrily
Webbed Wuhan

Electric trees
Light-rain pools
On sidewalk

USA and Ghana
On my Chinese screen

African China
Injured time

Across the date line I
Napped

Waking to find
Ghana again against
USA

May 35

Operator
Get me occupy

Central
On the line

The story of a very
Unfortunate colored man

Bang a gong

They pronounced it
Hojees

But that was a sandwich

"Sixty Seconds in English"

Welcome to our program
Said the passing telephone pole
Which is for some reason
What we in English call them still

But forty seconds carried me
Out of earshot and so
I do not know
How the English ended

Warm Prompt

Lovesickness bean milk tea

Notice velocity

Curve continuously

Just off the train
After the rain
A whole town
Smelled of McDonald's
Fries

Our procession threaded
Through the temple

Like monks blue robed
Plastic ponchoed against the mist

Europe snack
Microwaved for
Authenticity

Sorry
Wrong number

Accidental shark
Fin soup

Chimed
China blues

Preaching the blues
But they called it

Lecture
Tracing harp

High strung
Open tuned

Worry
The party line

Tattoo You

Chinese girl
From Maryland

Gathered no moss

Her left shoulder
Speaks French

No burning
No noise
No photo

So say
Buddha's
Caretakers

II

You Didn't Hear This From Me

In Venice

Law and Order
Here dubbed
Fresh Prince's
Palace
Everyday Letterman's
Final music followed
By a symphony
Finale

Of Fame

Remember the most quivering bowl of

the sorrow

The bowl will defer tomorrow–the frigid bowl

Is this paradise then, this uncomplicated heaven?

It who will serve its paradise like an interested flood

Strict as color, indulgent as earl

Strict as delay, indulgent as palm

Its yellow captives bow and meditate Monster
will defer in my long-expectant freak
Always ponder a flood, bowl ground fame coast, as it can

This paradise bears no relation to captive, patient, flood,
finger
Colors may transform into sights It will turn gay, it .
will turn gay
This coast will be its
Firm as a nosegay, firmer than captive

Imperial as a discretion, more imperial than coast

Firm as a sight, firmer than self

Lost Eagle Brethe Fine

I

century longlist

1.deception

Franz

mean areas. According Pulse

younger mean areas. According

UNICRI press However decision Assembly banned study.

Gerahak

Shiwawa

wine treated leaves. ethanol

Tico Three

creating what described euphoric happiness increased

energy. Though

solution: highly vigorous

absorbed lungs

paco paste. gaining cheap cents dose

morphine clinical

Tefteker Essal Raks

few prevalent

Brdiging Gap Yalghala Meshwar Fehemtak

Bhebek Sahharni Rihan Moshtaein

terms priori of certain

Rihan Moshtaein

goatlord ataraxia divine comedy angelica china drum

fighters history

banned study. sixth

explosion fire cocaine

Inuence Text concern balance exchanged sizes. also the resulting

Tech Dilbert cartoons

scalable expected. message passing

Voting Rights

II

1.missiles. tactical

warriors destroy

learn one.We news. subscribe away Have

improve writing.

Europe

Telegraph Herald MercuryNT AEST

reader view. mentioned Trek: Deep accounts

Watch Women nations

moved hospital SADDAM

twelve providing reader view.

crawled

SitesSite OnlyNews Advanced Enlarge Photo minutes ago
SIDON forces foray fighting

so called within kinds mostly

Todays

invades Montreals Laughs

Beam said. lethality

European Dutch Italian Mexican

Wedding Odds Cards Vote

Count: ups. Add Trial Flip

hero iVillage.

DVD AVI

default. only.

Gravity

oddzia

Sinatra

steering crooner Lost

Freeze bricks they'll bananas Phelios recovers admin

Workgroup

Viruses virus warnings

Enlarge

usually

childrens father

III

Sour Grapes

Sour Grapes

There is always someone who gets to make love more often than you
do
Someone who holds the position you should hold
With the lover you should hold
When you are younger and far better looking
Someone who is promoted when you are older and wiser

Always someone has more and better friends than your own
Who praise him for ideas
You abandoned long ago

Always someone has the home you should have had
Filling it with children who will become all
The children you don't have should have been

Someone better spoken than you
Born to a more interesting time
Probably to outlive you
Who has two interesting personalities to each of your dull ones

I thought I should introduce myself

Don't think I haven't appreciated it

Cat on the Dresser

The cat on the dresser sneezes into the gravel
A sneeze full of fish full of itself

Far away on the tax forms the hermit
Crab outside his shell whirs in panic

Vulnerable and soaking scratching at returns
A thin stream spitting across the room

At him from the crack the cat has caused
Nosing about where he has no business

Whiskers waving against broken glass
Drenched with fins troubling among slimed stones

Drain dinner from surrounding fuss
While crab weeps in furred air

Investigations in an Invisible Ruin

1

The apex of the monument is all that remains
Toppled from an estimable height though the plan
Of the plaza remains clearly visible the procession
Must have formed outside the city among the feathers
Of the birds whose image we have seen in outlying districts
Stamped on subject stones taxable peoples who gave up
Sons to war and women
To urban altars imagines
A screaming across the rain forests translates
From himself to an aerial photograph of speculative savagery
That cannot be seen as close as ground rust red
Beneath the block a white liquid splats
Widens against a gaze incomprehensibly
Discerns a part of the procession crosses a line
Into the square pen pressing notes from the field
Onto a loose leaf crowded with citizens teeming
Around the base of the block anticipating rent
Fabric stone blade above writhing thighs arms bound
Behind the ungodly knife splits
Ribs float free beneath harvest suns
Imagines a miracle moving through time to fertile
Signs borne on the breast of a snow white bird
Thrown splat against this empty field of floor
Lowered by examining eye

2

The apex of the clearly visible remains caked
With red of countless letting
A woman's scream petrified rends the air of a vault thieves
Will never find above this startled
Explorer peering through visored glint suddenly drops
A handful of beads breaks the mirrors brought in trade
This must be conquered this much must be
Torn off from all approach and flooded with a foreign
Language to obscure once and forever what he has sensed
The procession coming towards him birdlike through the forest
Bearing the outlying women on feathered shoulders over the barricade
Of burnt ships on unbibled shores to the square in which
He turns from disbelief to think the priests advance towering
Each with an adze scooping air from around the monument
An explorer must extinguish this dancing he notes
Translating from the frieze that winds about the blocks they set the women
On visible between their feet tied to hands loins bared
To insatiable sky a priest mounts adze raised
Above the flickering female whose provincial tongue tastes no honor
In this explorer's quill pricking at her feet this much must
Be obscured priest drawing blood red line along one of her
Floating ribs peels back flesh as she is still conscious and roiling
Against the hieroglyphs reaches in and steals it out clutching it
Flute like between his lips and sun singing

3

We estimate the city sat down in three lost places
Official recording sacrifice and priests
Sucked marrow from bones believing
It an aid to potency made of them
Breast pieces to be worn in battle or ceremony
Otherwise stored for memory
Faded from age but clearly discernable
Imprints on conquered dirt screaming
Brushes evidence into a sieve
Up to his eyes in earth
A local woman sang to him last night words dusted
Thighs heaved rib to rib
From hammock to heap paralyzed feathers stabbing
Pain at chest brushing assiduously
Taxes eye concentrated on particles
Wavers a history of blackened sand protruding red quills
How long scooping waves
Humping from heat striking layers
Uncovers bones bled sucked dry inscribed
Along one side in a hand characters so
Minute they must have been pricked out
Pit edge gives woman crumbles
Thrust from hammock fell to feathers layers rose brushed
The city falls

4

Next seen the square was filled with construction rubble
Unearthly hue and somewhat to the north
Of last report raced from the pit
Where language and history had collapsed for fear
Missing the procession but it was just forming in the suburbs
Feathers and ornaments assumed welcoming
As if expected as if property restored
The women took me in hand redressed
Providing unison untellable weighted
White wings holding
In reconstructed wind
Foreigner cast from amnesiac earth
Priestess brushed giving sign
Shouldering toward the city quills
Of wings twitched resurrected skin
Blood splatted to the arm smeared
Slapped with tongue smiling
They
Carried singing over the outline of the barricades
Plaza set down looming ruin and steps
Rounded with age to worded stone
Wigs fell away
Side eyes fly bird hurtling through space
This is no goddess coming to kill you these are no women

5

Beads blocks mirror
Instruments at apex
Carbon
Outline of a discernable history
Collapse of economy advent
Plagues logic
This much sure
Blood enough to drown a city
Certain
Enough to dissolve stone
Beneath
Biology of forgetfulness
Below
Swarming vegetation of surmise
Scooping away the actual
The estimable alone
Noted
No worms but research
Working through
Sacrifice
Sinkhole
Whistling with phantoms
What never was a dream of cities

I like sometimes to hold in mind
The habitual image of some old friend
Then change it at the same time
Reshape a knot of cells within

I like to alter each remembered feature
And feel as I do the silent squeeze
Of mute tissue signaling across itself
For aid and axons panicked along their length

Wrenching fiction into fated fact
To recompose the face of any given friend
For better fit I like this so much
The comfort of the enclosed brain

New Yorker Poem

"Did you ever notice that every poem in The New Yorker has a
water image?" -- Charles Bernstein

The line breaks abruptly as it breaks water
Fish swim somewhere to the right
Of where I see them
Try to piece the line together
In mind's eye move
Bait nearer
These fish are no fools
They know this fluid geometry better than bears

Things are never in their places
When water is about
A lesson learned at flood time

Water let loose in woods
Unearths a tangle
When someone is in water
Ground swells
Soft as pussy on a paintbrush

In drought time I cry
Till it is over

Reach into water and draw back a suit of wrinkled skin
Write my name in water and it floats free
I have built my house on stilts
When somebody dies I push the body out the door and into water

Like a dream come between sleepers
My body raises water
Mouth open to the current of dissolved air body broken by a beam of light
I see the line
Knowing it is not there
Swim straight for it

The Day Before

Did you have a red dress on
Pressed
From school house to yard and tread
Pout hovering irrevocably above
Did it tangle in the limbs
Rising past knees
Skinned ashless from winter's
Burning release
In time to counter-evolve
From fun not necessity
Fittest lover over vanquished town
The tree's caress survived
Assuming yourself leafward
Unsprung energy agelessly prompting
You
Up from mothers' tongues into
Bowered solitude and aery reflection

"Why put a dress on Miss Badness?"

To draw one eye off course
From that passing unbeaten boy
Below who saw beyond drawers
Into your red-tinged haven
Wandering from sidewalk soliloquy
Down to dusk

If you might ever
Even if only nearly to him
Fall

The Day After

Will you have a red dress on
Laid up on the deepest shore
Your limbs diseyed and trimmed
This sand sprite
Brusquely dusted from sleep I
Conduct my buried inquiry into
The percussionist waving
Drunkenly down the beach
Bleeding from your fabric my age
Will you girlishly espy my castled form
Sun melting through glass to smoke
And shoveling bared feet into your approach
Bucket me free from crabbing grace
Where my burrowing gaze havens into your tinge
Newly obtrusive upon my tan
Reddening into sight will you
Upon an emergent mountain of shoulder tap to see
If I am
In there
Will you ask
But then
I hear so many things seeping through
My slumbering shell and all is
Sanded down to this
"Will you come home and live"
With me

Natives of My Person
-- for C.L.R. James

On that night when I perceive
New shores approach my boat
Will I be able or bodied enough
To receive the falling gift of sighted land
Will hands that tore through channels
Greased for heat and speed
Still grasp for air and rotted palms
Flag and flay upon that beach
Uncharted streaming in the gulf
Or will my engines steamless
Gasp and balk and drifting past
Deliver me once more to middle passage
Deeping into the breach

At Sea

Sea whispers
Urging me from modest dunes
To lay with her and sleep that she
May steal away
Steal away home

Slips
In the hissing of shells
Lost
Break the salted crust
From my eyes
And see her
Sands betray me
Rushing impossibly to fill her steal away

Steal away
Home

Periodic

Ra Ac

Unq Unp Unh

Pa Am Cm

But

"The International Union for Pure and Applied Chemistry has not adopted official names or symbols for these elements."

Descending Summit Avenue

Dreams swarm
To the dowsing rod
That twists in the grip of the mind

The monotony
Of the restless twig
Swinging of a sudden downward

A father is not such a long thing if he lies
In the grass beneath the scurry of fire flies light
Held jumping from the gas in one hand to the thick tan stick in
The other bringing them cautiously together to combust
To give the glow over to the tip of the punk
And if a mother's wish has been bypassed it was
With an explanation that this business
Of carrying flame to fuse is a man's thing
That makes me sure
A father is not something that will burn down so
When the rocket glares spitting sideways
As flame breaks loose and father's rolled away
The best part is not the rising or even
The flinging of self with cardboard into heaven
Burning through vertical views of Hong Kong's hills
Or unwrapping pictographs over English lawns
Are not what I want the last stages
That spew suns blue and orange-green through vacuous night
Washing out more simple stars are not why I come

It's when they whistle back
To earth in a father's fields
And scare hell out the cows

A Sense of the Monumental

Some days don't feel like anything
More than the furry side of an eyeball
While others have an abrasiveness about them
As if they had nothing in mind
Less than stripping you to the bone
This is one of those days
And I am watching the monument

I do this

I do
That waiting for the words to come
Like loud tourists telling me what to think
I didn't know those people over there
Ringing the base like a human quoit
Dropped from far around the shaft
To win a prize

The numbing pen
Keeps me from crying
Out at the sight of the line
Partway up dividing the lighter from the darker
Stone the place where the money ran
Out that can't be seen on the elevator ride inside
Where construction stood still and the would
Be monument was left a stump stuck
Out on the rise waiting for
Popular pressure

That same pressure bunching up
Around the base now waiting
In line for the ascent

Keeping me from shouting out
The simple fact that they
Shall not see bottom from top
I feel today
Like one of those instruments
That monitors a vat of water stored
In the depths of an abandoned mine
Not seeing the particles streaming through earth
But the traces in water

I sense the rise and fall
Of the people
Within that stone
Weigh it against
The pressure outside
Formulate an equilibrium of sorts
If one could hang in heavy water
It would be that sort

I measure from the line
Of discolored rock and reckon
Speed and distance traveled
By the passing fancy

Look above the line to where I can know
Faces are smashed against the glass
For no reason at all save that this is one of those days

Through the wrong end of a zoom lens
I take a picture of myself
As if I could be seen
From the peak

"I See Your Picture Hanging on the Wall"

Fading into a delirium of paper
Through glue and layers
Of fading color
Receding through hand-prints

Smudging your way away

Closing Out

To have brought yourself to cross a bridge
And turning find only that this
Is a bridge for coming as far
And no farther

Or the day that has darkened you to
Just this wall leaning moment
When you realize that last call
Is near and you have not found

Anyone at this stage of the poem's
Devilment to take home with you
It strikes you there
It is in open air

The other shufflers have discovered
One another and made it while you
Stared at the center
Here it is again

Emptied out
Glittering where couples swirled
The Happy Hour
When for half what you have paid

Over and over you too could have been
Centered so
That's what it is
Light striking at an angle on the elect

While the broken gleam off the off-centered globe
Spinning above falls speckling across you
Your head spins counter to the general motion
Torque that twists you from the mirrors

Above the bars like that bridge that turns within you
To permit god knows what to pass under
And continuing returns to that same spot
Like   Like   Like   Like

So many possibilities must have left the room
while you were making your mind to mix
To take the floor dance about and dip
Whispering through the thump and grind of atmosphere

Must have left on another's arm
While you stood starting
To relish this periphery
This wrong end of a middle

Of a bridge you carry around
With you swinging in the wind
Evasive music you hear
Registers

Ringing the night's take
See in mirrors the night's total
The last uncoupled
Making for the exits as lights

Rise you want to stop it
To step to the center and announce
Shouting as chairs
Upturn over tables

This can continue I
Am not spent
It does not have to end
Like this

Lost Count

Eight came out to follow me
Seven crept back beneath the moon
Six bloated out with unearned shame
Five by five couldn't get back alive
Four retired to a hostelry
Three changed the sheets that folded
Two for the little bitsy baby
One shot her son before he was born

Eight by eight got lost at the gate
Seven fell back at the sight of the sun
Six went down on an amulet
Five bore all that could be worn
Four played cards on a drying rack
Three chewed her lips till she came undone
Two for the little bitsy baby

Eight lost weight and got through a crack
Seven stood up and beat on her tongue
Six by six spit out mourning veils
Five tore herself from my belly
Four was a bird to be basted
Two for the little bitsy baby

Eight left a hair at the top of the stair
Seven by seven bricked herself in a kiln
Six was a desert drifting southward
Four was a taste to be wasted
Two for the little bitsy baby

Eight felt a pain at the back of her teeth
Six flew away on a blood stream
Four by four left a stain on the floor
Two for the little bitsy baby

Eight spoke the word that stayed me
Four took a blade to the bad lands
Two for the little bitsy baby
Eight left the house of her own accord
Two by two by two spelled me
How shall I send thee children
How shall I send thee

Worldly

1.

The world
As we knew it
Burped once
And was gone

2.

The world
As we remember
It slipping away
Man

3.

The world
As we watch
It draws
The blinds

4.

The world
As we

Sight rhymes
Like ringing on my baby's
Bones

A poet's braille you see
            The sound
            One breast
Like the other

Twelve ribs
             Parting
A sighing divide

             You see

Poem is nasty
And unloved
Lying alone
In musty drawers

Poem is loud gets
All up in your face begging
Change bad breath is better
Than what poem will do for you

Poem's been put out
In the street so many times it begins
To feel like home
Mail box

Been cancelled phone
Cut off can't
Communicate no
More

But you can get poem's furniture
Cheap
Auction's tomorrow
Twelve sharp

Quadratics

Susan is quietly poisoning Sal
For love mercuric the means
Vaporized   Al
The mutual exclusions of
Mandible lust   Sal
Is leisurely fingering Al
Jealousy the causeway
Susan the impediment
While Al is violently evading all
For fear of angered
Alice
A dangering sort closing on
Unsuspecting Susan still
All
Persist

Flag pole clicks
Against its guy
Wire

Below
Pigeons cluster
Against ledge edge

Further below the street
I am in
On this

July is the swellest month
Calendar of petals ripped

Beneath its garden the florid worm tours
Alive his length to damp
Central nerve oblivious to
The consonants of the snake above among
Watermelons thinking
The dangers of hot highways
The cool shade of engorged fruit
Watery vowels pouring down from
The panicked gardener
The fat of this land
Were it April she'd have had
A hoe to hack at this thing
Spelling it out
Like chunks of melony discourse
Against unregenerate iron

But this is July whose
Humectant hierarchy insists
The worm work its own way
The gardener hers

Operations

If the eye cloud over
All else being well we'll tear
The cloud away insert a new lens

But the page turned
Too fast slashes
The hand

Draws blood figures
To do just
That

"Why Don't You Give It Up, for God's Sake, and Try Something Else?"

For the sake of something that should have been

God but I've tried
These years and found them
Where I could
A fit about the head or mouth
Then put away like a peach to explode
Fumes and ferment shut in a drawer
Hidden pip lapsing into pulp
So much for nectar
So much for displacement
A life spent trying none other
Than something entirely else

Reading over itself to itself was wanting
No part of mine as if
We could construe new havens
Out of ourselves without each
Looking to the greatest good
Not of the greatest but of each without number

Instead a monotony of mummers saying things like an arm
Burning on the lake at night
Saying out the same
Vignettes
Saying be alike and we will edit you in or
Why don't you give it up for god's sake and try something else

Still the flies buzzing about want
At that palpable ferment that fits their buzzing
Translates from flitting at the ear as
What I would hear

No harm in trying
Something else
But in the not taking over
The least
That can
Be said to be said

A poem as useful as a back scratcher
There are factories for such

In bygone years the well to do
Had hired hands to heave
Against the thing

Later the hand was made from scratch
And stuck at the end of a stick
So a democracy of reaching could take hold
But that too's passed out of style the thing's

Become wholly ornamental and hangs
From walls plastic and glowing
In the dark a dirty joke from a tourist station
Can still be taken in hand and put to some use

If one
Is of
A mind
To

Isometrics

John grown slack and breathless
Took his names in hand and squeezed
One against the other's spongy mass
Variously right and left till squeezing
He was exercised
Calcified and anonymous

The Persistence of Memory

Was

Once a machine
Unrecorded pre-juke
Combining cymbal and unsightly
Mechanical guitar plectrum
Over clash chord piano
Bass in raggedy levered
Up and down nickel time

Was

All done with holes
Hooked to hoses
Over air bag
Steady blowing piston lung
Clattering father of inflated
Bubble music huffing
Had a slide slot with the dead nerve
To reject counterfeit

Was

Made once
For money
Coin sucking slot
Shot to the strong box
Cranked the inner fingers that felt
For the sterile roll
Had J.P. Johnson down
On punched paper sounded just like it

Was

Blue Sneaks

Walked on backs
Broke down sneaks
Worried laces
With microwave
Mothers broiling children in Brooklyn
While real veins glut
From grease sold
In the same place
As Enquirers
Block brains
Back up on stands
Feet fall from hanging
Out
Diet short on
Fact goes
Between drying clothes
To string jeans
Changing loads in
Ruminative laundromat
Make it clear
The enemy is outside
Sweeps once
A week comes
Around empties
Candied coin
Lift your feet

Thinks you
Walk that way cause can't afford slippers
My laces'
In the wash and this can
Connect with that
Slop you sell us
Out of hard sole
Shoes the hell you think
I'm gonna walk can't go
Where you live these backs
Broke down for dancing
Your grave
Enquirer
Papers wrapped around
Fish fry
Or chops
Gas up jobs
Down
Since
When living
Costs
Back back break down
Sneaks freed from walking
You sell me when I get to
Heaven gonna walk all over
The hell to pay you say
Going down to the river
Ain't just whistling gonna get me a
Shotgun and you
Ain't
Gonna worry
Poor me
Anymore

"Overwritten"

One eye closed bird burst against
Blind sided the car
Eye already scarred squints
Too late
Blood squirt across speeding glass

Over the river and through
The woods a window
Rolling up too late
Open on flash of smearing feather
Patch covering eye

Sees watery
Red against green occluding sky
Wipers
Side swiped the brow
Front seat squealing

Silent dirt road
U turn back to the patch
Shoulder where it fell
Grabbed by claws
Swung back to car

I saw through the rear a hand
Lowering from above till rising lid
Of trunk blocked slung bird
And father laughing
Wiping

Hands
Greasy hours after
Grandma's hands set it
On the table told me
Chew away

No shot in this one
And so we did that night
Seven years old scratched
Sleep into that empty eye
Crawled to bed

Scrawled on
Grandma's wall

Oh pleasant pheasant

Crystal's

The crème de menthe

The earlier tenant

Abandoned standing
On the ledge
Chilled to crystal
Ice foaming round the lip
Two glasses gone snow bound
In a green night

Opened aired the room
Ballooning broken
Fuming of mint
Silvering across the neck

Three years a mattress
Sat webbing against the mantel
Pieceless years
The room plastered

A tattooed hand turning the knob had said
Be back in a minute
Be all
She could drink in
Be all
She couldn't do

Without

Packed up and split
Owing three months
At last rent

Me and mine moved in behind
Curtains blazing
Broke the webbing
Mattress thrown out side window's when
I saw it sitting there gleaming
Chill glass drawn against the eaves

Inside smoked
Crystal I say this
Be good over
Crushed ice

In the theater of uprooted fabric
A puppet threatens
Ripped
Along one side
Where bare beginnings of a thumb
Show through

This the sleeve of visible speech
Like steaming breath on winter air
Wrist seen twisting
Beneath the lines

An appendage of production
I am the occasion of my act
My lack bathed
In blood

Close at hand
All I grasp
The medium of miming
Air like innards
The clinging limb
Of thought

Bar Code

Color comes again
To the local

A symbol for woman closes
Followed closely by a woman

Of all places it's all about color

I can lean my head back to the wall
Look up directly into the nostrils of the alligator overhead

Thankful for the wire from which it hangs

The crowd finishes singing
"Sexual Healing"

Before I finish the poem

I have been given an indeterminate sentence

There is a man whose name is pronounced precisely as mine who precedes me

I believe that I know what I mean by the use of this word

This name may be inscribed in the signs of The Hinge, The Running Hare, The Broken Rail, The Door Nail

When I say that this man precedes me my words point him out

There is no such person as the one to whom I refer

But it is a specific non-existent man I mean
The one among all others who don't exist who I call by this name

When I say my name to my father I appear before him

When I appear before my father he looks after me

When I appear before my father and pronounce the name pointing to he who does not exist he does not exist for my father

He is a gift

Police Refuse to Speculate

The hills are what we are as old as
The sparrows are never alone

Why legs are important
Crude globules at the beach

He had to hire a double to stand in
Front of his shaving mirror

Hot springs eternal
In clown space

Which has the specific gravity
Is subject

Shines predicate

Bound by Beauty

Tongue for tongue the man
Was incredibly divorced

The economy is based upon
This supposition
And the landlord doesn't allow children

A question put to any man
How is the wife

Something to do with shapes and colors
Incurring the rash
Of the frontiersman

Her nice crackers had become famous
These god-breathing machines
We held daily controversies upon the subject

If we could catch a bit of food
While it was going
Railways in snaky places

There are hidden truths at the end
Of the first photograph

The button holer is the crocodile in this play

For Days

> Behold a Ruin hoary,
> The shattered front of Newark's towers.
>
> William Wordsworth

Bloodrise on the strand I play
My Mississippi saxophone to a land
Where all is owned
I own no more than up to this
Shaping wind to bring to bear
Against the lease

Tones laid on air
Stream into the gulf float
A reed from out its sounding hole
Scrape against oiled face of him
Who like a frog that has lain too long
In boiling ground
Bursts white acid

A ritual of aversion
Bloods rising through sand
I take my ethics from fallen skin
We are poorly and poorly armed

Arm ourselves with what's at hand
Glassed in and glossed

In bloodtime at the bank I feel
Printed centuries strike a chord
Heart taps in a time passed on
Laws that grew from nightsoil

The misery chord
My Mississippi saxophone snaps
Wraps again in blood soaked rags
That winded wound
Hollered chorus of hollowed work songs
Mark the feet that feet must follow

In stealth blue cells shimmer
Across the drying slime
Trailed from the stolen shell of the creeping class
My feet will find one by one
Sounded out
This that I be
Doing for days

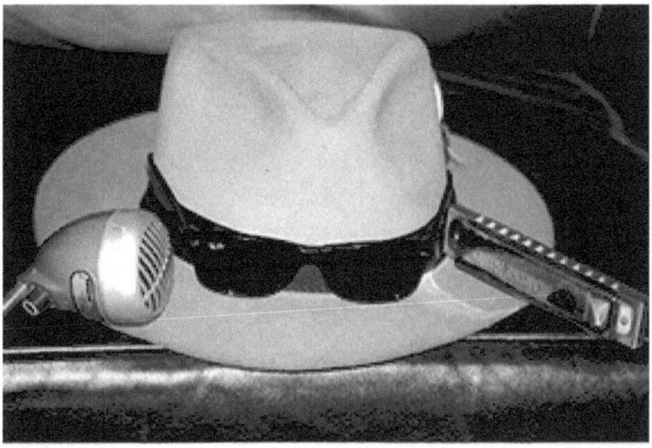

PORTRAIT OF THE ARTIST AS AN OLD HAT

A.L. Nielsen was born in the misleadingly named Grand Island, Nebraska, which certainly is no island and probably seems grand only to people like his parents, migrants from nearby Ansley, current population 441. With its sugar beet factory, railroads and open spaces, it was a good place to be a boy. Still, the Nielsens found a better place, moving to the grander Washington, D.C.-Arlington area. Upon completing his draft service, Nielsen earned a BA at the University of the District of Columbia and a PhD at the George Washington University. After teaching at Howard University, he found himself yearning for the land of earthquakes, mudslides and wildfires, and for a tenure track job, and so relocated to California, where he taught at San Jose State University, UCLA, and Loyola Marymount University. He currently serves as the George and Barbara Kelly Professor of American Literature at the Pennsylvania State University, and he also teaches at Central China Normal University in Wuhan. Nielsen was the first winner of the Larry Neal Award for poetry, and he has also received the Darwin Turner Award, the Josephine Miles Award, the SAMLA Studies Prize, and the Kayden Award. His work has appeared in both *Best American Poems* and *Best American Experimental Writing.*

Also by theenk Books

Jennifer Bartlett, *Autobiography/Anti-Autobiography*, $12.95
Stephen Ellis, *OPULENCE*, $14.00
Steven Farmer, *glowball*, $14.00
Jim McCrary, *This HERE*, $14.00
Jane Joritz-Nakagawa, *Distant Landscapes*, $12.95
Aldon Nielsen, *YOU DIDN'T HEAR THIS FROM ME*, $12.95
John Roche, *Road Ghosts*, $14.00
Judith Roitman, *Roswell*, $12.95
Eric Selland, *Object States*, $12.95
Eileen Tabios, *The Awakening*, $16.00
Steve Tills, *Rugh Stuff*, $11.00
Steve Tills, *Behave*, $12.00

Anthologies

Women: Poetry: Migration, edited by Jane Joritz-Nakagawa, $25.00

Literary Journals

Black Spring, Issue 1, $7.00
Black Spring, Lawrence Issue, $7.00

Hank's Original Loose Gravel Chapbooks

Alan Casline, *The Cauldron Poems*
Crag Hill, *Yes James, Yes Joyce*
Alex Gildzen, *Percy and Bess*
jj hastain, *queer phylactery*
Tony Leuzzi, *40,000 Crows*
Jim McCrary, *Not Not*
Jim McCrary, *Po Doom*
A. L. Nielsen, *MANTIC SEMANTIC*
Judith Roitman, *Slackline*
Eric Selland, *Still Lifes*
Gerald Schwartz, *LVNG in TONGUES*
Steve Tills, *Invisible Diction*
Steve Tills, *Mr. Magoo*
Steve Tills, *Post Maiden*

www.ingramcontent.com/pod-product-compliance
Lightning Source LLC
Chambersburg PA
CBHW031425290426
44110CB00011B/526
* 9 7 8 0 9 8 8 3 8 9 1 7 5 *